Dissolve in Fire,
then Blend

DISSOLVE IN FIRE, THEN BLEND

The Hermetic Gallery of Word-Paintings
and Symbolic Prayers to the Cosmic Mind

*with a few accompanying
photographs and illustrations*

Daniel de la Fé

Phoenix Pyre Publishing
2019

First published by Phoenix Pyre Publishing
First Edition: September, 2019
Printed in the United States of America

Cover art: *Silent Treatise on the Nature of the Soul,*
oil on canvas, by the author, 2019.

Book design by the author,
with assistance by Katelyn Kopenhaver.

Photographs and illustrations on
pgs. 9, 14, 24, 29, 40, 49, 57, 66 by the author.

Engraving on pg. 74 from
Das Narrenshiff (Ship of Fools)
by Sebastian Brant, printed in Basel, 1596.

Photograph of the author by Katelyn Kopenhaver:
Fifth Story Window Overlooking
57th St. and 10th Ave. Hell's Kitchen, April 2019.

ISBN-10: 0-578-56122-0
ISBN-13: 978-0-578-56122-6

For my future Self.
Whoever you become, I have Faith
that you will look back upon these works
and these years without *too much* guilt or shame;
that they will serve as a reminder of where you
have been, how far you have come, and where
you may still have to go in the end. Look
back only to *remember*, never to *dwell*.

And to the brilliant painter,
Roger González de la Red,
for reminding me that True
Art is created to honor
the Divine.

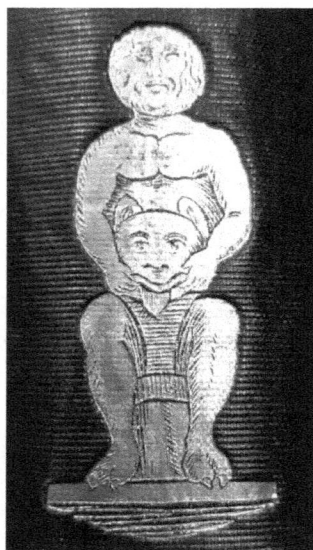

GALLERY LISTING

"'We have already spoken about the meaning of being 'born'. This relates to the beginning of a new growth of essence, the beginning of the formation of individuality, the beginning of the appearance of one indivisible I.

"But in order to be able to attain this or at least begin to attain it, a man must die, that is, he must free himself from a thousand petty attachments and identifications which hold him in the position in which he is. He is attached to everything in his life, attached to his imagination, attached to his stupidity, attached even to his sufferings, possibly to his sufferings more than to anything else. He must free himself from this attachment. Attachment to things, identification with things, keep alive a thousand useless I's in a man. These I's must die in order that the big I may be born. But how can they be made to die? They do not want to die. It is at this point that the possibility of awakening comes to the rescue. To awaken means to realize one's nothingness, that is to realize one's complete and absolute mechanicalness and one's complete and absolute helplessness. And it is not sufficient to realize it philosophically in words. It is necessary to realize it in clear, simple, and concrete facts, in one's own facts.

"When a man begins to know himself a little he will see in himself many things that are bound to horrify him. So long as a man is not horrified at himself he knows nothing about himself. A man has seen in himself something that horrifies him. He decides to throw it off, stop it, put an end to it. But however many efforts he makes, he feels that he cannot do this, that everything remains as it was. Here he will see his impotence, his helplessness, and his nothingness; or again, when he begins to know himself a man sees that he has nothing that is his own, that is, that all that he has regarded as his own, his views, thoughts, convictions, tastes, habits, even faults and vices, all these are not his own, but have been either formed through imitation or borrowed from somewhere ready-made. In feeling this a man may feel his nothingness. And in feeling his nothingness a man should see himself as he really is, not for a second, not for a moment, but constantly, never forgetting it.

"This continual consciousness of his nothingness and of his helplessness will eventually give a man the courage to 'die,' that is, to die, not merely mentally or in his consciousness, but to die in fact and to renounce actually and forever those aspects of himself which are either unnecessary from the point of view of his inner growth or which hinder it. These aspects are first of all his 'false I,' and then all the fantastic ideas about his 'individuality,' 'will,' 'consciousness,' 'capacity to do,' his powers, initiative, determination, and so on.'"

—Gurdjieff, from *In Search of the Miraculous: Fragments of an Unknown Teaching*, P.D. Ouspensky, pg. 218

Dissolve in Fire, then Blend

Dissolve
in Fire.
Blend
these
pieces
in the Heat.
Here, cook *yourself.*
In a Giant Flask, we are
ingredients for an Experiment
higher than our understanding:
a Working from the Source.
Remember this prayer by
remembering yourself
in each moment,

or at least
by making an attempt,
to then feel the friction
of *fission* initiate.

Flames

leap into   *the Sky*

as our being   leaps into

this one body,   inhabiting it;

bodies that in-   habit homes,

as these houses   inhabit this

big planet; this   planet in this

great galaxy;   this galaxy,

inside this *uni-*   *verse*; this

*uni*verse in a   Cosmos; be

-ings made *of,*   made *from,*

composing a   Single Entity,

of which each   of us springs,

a Stream   *flowing*

into Soil.

Marriage at Cana

Dark
blue hue into
a teal-aquamarine
marries the subtle orange
with pink, the sea of sky trans-
forming into a fine rosé, like the
hand of Christ turning water into

spirits to quench the Spirit's thirst.
Nocturne, composed and painted.
Last glimpse; He nods farewell
to another day, like the trains
that pass away while we sit
on a platform of existence
at the Elizabeth Station,
having to choose a
Middle Path.
Sun of
Man
soon departs
after the miracle
is complete. We drink
this Wine, carried onward.

Rooftop Snapshot Reflection

My shadow-cast silhouette sinks into
the roof from which this frame stands,
a transient mark of a single fragmented
presence here on this Orb in Your Hand,
expertly etched by the Autumn Sun—
peering down along 57th Street,
drinking in the flowing movements of
other versions of itself swimming along:
consuming, feeling, thinking,
growing, gaining, glowing, gliding,
learning, losing... dreaming...
numbing, forgetting, plotting, scheming,
loving, *fooling themselves*, dying.
This Season of Receding renews me—
reaping, threshing, winnowing
the components of my corporeal flask.

The voice you now hear in your head
was in that shadow, *watching*.
That shadow was an inkwell.

Gorgoneion

Cast a gaze upon those of malintention. Hear this:
"Don't assume I can't see you lurking nearby—that you
could just slither through my door, overestimating an
ease of predation, underestimating finding your own
inner mask looking back at you—*freeze!* Keep your
distance if you hunger for an easy feast; you'll come
to greet Athena's Shield before Her Spear seeks!
I have my own inner demons to contend
with here and no time to spare
on parasites."

So I speak it: *"Mal de Ojo, cast your gaze elsewhere!"*
Become the one who senses with an inner *nazar*
which strikes first, yet strategically, humbly,
and True. She will guide our hand as
it holds the lantern up—holds
up the Apotropaic Light
to reveal!

Cast a gaze upon malintention inside myself. Hear this:
"Sever the head of your inner Medusa then hold it up
to the eroded grotesques guarding the walls of your
Laboratorial Cathedral. Discerningly admit
only those who are deserving of it!"

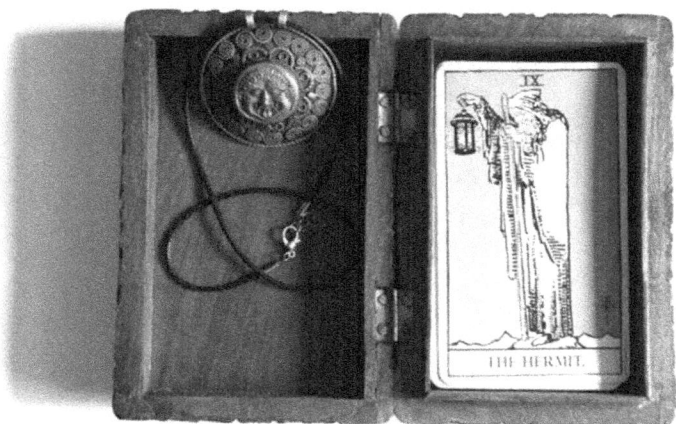

Another Putrefaction:
Mat: 27:50

It's unclear what drove me to walk in here on my way
home on this cold December night, with bags of groceries in hand. I pass by every week, never entering;
grew up with its steeple watching over us, bells ringing
across Quality Hill. I *do* recall wandering in here a few
years prior, through the back entrance on Race Street
(the way I used to enter with my grandmother)—only
peeking in for a moment at the glowing windows during
the day. It was beautiful, as churches often are when full
of light. The impact is much different at night.

The process of growth always requires periods of
absolute darkness before gestation or germination. This
time I entered through the front doors by the light of the
Moon. I've attempted the front doors before and they
were always locked. Tonight they opened up for me.

An aroma of waxed wooden pews. Figure, nailed
thrice above the altar, *centered* in a golden triptych,
accepting His fate, with a winged angel on each side.
INRI above His head. Waves strike, filling my mouth
with salt water stopping words until sitting. The church,
dimly lit, Her stained glass an opaque Silent Veil. A
single Latina woman stood before the altar, praying
quietly in Spanish.

Steps echoing softly, I found a row in the middle—a
seat on the end to the right, setting my groceries down.
Quite a few years had come and gone since having set

foot in here; on the surface, everything was the same as I remember as a child.

Held back sudden emergence of salt water seeping from my own stained glass windows, immediately thinking, *Such an emotional response all initiated by a smell. It is* melancholy, *exactly. Maybe a drop of divine desperation? Fear? Uncertainty? Discontent with my-self? All wrapped up in impressions here with grandma and my brother, from childhood to 15-years-old, when I stopped coming—stopped believing. Even when I sort of returned to 'believing,' I did not 'believe' in quite the same way anymore. Now I see something I could not then....*

Another Latina woman walks in, doors creaking closed behind her as she passed me down the center aisle before stopping beside the first woman. A momentary time travel back to when Irish immigrants once stood where they stood, sat where I sat when the church was founded in 1844 and looked much more ornate inside; another to eating those stale crackers, sipping watered down wine; confessions with Monsignor Harrington, and how many Hail Mary's to say; to sitting here almost every Sunday, from a little boy to angsty-adolescence, sometimes paying attention to the sermons, but often daydreaming, staring up and analyzing the windows and idols, or making up stories in my head in far-off strange places. Once I finally grew up, the strangeness of Reality far out-weighed what I could imagine or read in fantasy books… the strangeness of God's Mind. And sometimes I feel, even for just fleeting moments, *outside of time.*

But what was this *peculiar phenomenon before me moving someone so deeply to tears, beyond rational*

11

understanding, stretching out through our perception of time? Or that brings these women to whispered prayers? Brings out my own silent prayers of desperation in ink? What are such impressions of the past, impressions left upon my being? And what is Truly behind it all?

Here I sit on the Winter Solstice, in St. Mary of the Assumption on Washington Avenue, near the end of one sun revolution and the beginning of another—still *here*, yet wandering inside—wondering what the next will possibly have in store for me and *how I will respond.* I look to the Star to steer my ship on this Ship of Fools.

It reminds me of a similar feeling once had, looking up at the night sky when I was once more naïve—that shaking tremble of being lost to find a Way....

It is that looking into the vastness of the unknown which keeps me sailing, strangely enough. As hard as it is to accept, I know in suffering intently we sacrifice for our future selves while serving others, and in serving *consciously* we create a Home around us. Maybe then we may confidently weigh our hearts against the *Feather of Ma'at* by never wasting the Gift of Thought, while trying to take care of our fragile temporal forms, for only this can help worthy hearts *see*, balance, and remain on course. We will greet the skeletal arms bearing the Scythe without this trembling, but as old friends, giving each and everything, everyone, every aspect of ourselves *the Name is it due* in the Name of THE KEEPER OF ALL NAMES.

After it all passes, in silence I have already prayed in my own way. Eyes dry. Words stop. Mind rests. Heart and body go still.

Strange fruit fallen to the Earth are those who truly *die with Him* intentionally*, bourn from Her eternal Womb within the Gift of the Present! Igne Natura Renovatur Integra,* perpetually. I write this with love, dear reader: pick up your Shovel and dig. Pick up your sword and slay the Ladon lurking at the base of Your Tree. His many trappings are ephemeral, yet what you will discover buried Down There, eternal! The seed inside all of this muck and grime, which cyclically raises, consumes, and digests beings and bodies up from the mud—that Seed is of the same Essence of what's Up There, manifest in golden fruit, glorious!

We'll conquer that when we conquer the Dragon in ourselves, untangling the hypnotic spell through this dark lair of *maya.*

In contemplative silence we Work and pray, Work and pray, Work and pray. Just remember to remind yourself that *stumbling is part of the Way!*

HAIL MARY, FULL OF GRACE,
THE LORD IS WITH THEE.
BLESSED ART THOU AMONGST WOMEN,
AND BLESSED IS THE FRUIT OF THY WOMB, JESUS.
HOLY MARY, MOTHER OF GOD,
PRAY FOR US SINNERS,
NOW AND *AT THE HOUR OF OUR DEATH,*
AMEN.

Yellow Cab

What is being 'alive,' if not
jumping into yellow cabs
with drivers who decide
to just go anywhere?
How many of us are really
behind our own wheel—
ever even *touched it once?*
Very few, I imagine.
Unseen forces pull us forward
or backwards or sideways
more often than we think.

automata feed

Cutting realization: the reflection in the mirror
which goes against the one I normally see
or want to see in my head—
the cutting reality we mostly munch,
to assuage an insatiable hunger, deep—
that the hand with which we reach
for help, or even to give help to others,
can do so with a buried intent to simply leech—
we constantly chase, desire, deceive ourselves,
even when we believe we are being heroic,
or that we're doing good for the world.
Carrying around our traumas and karmas
in a sack tied to a stick, thrown over our shoulder:
Damsel-in-Distress Complexes,
White Knight Syndromes, Manipulation Protocols,
projecting all the muck and grime onto
every interaction, every moment—
disassociation—fleeing silence with ourselves,
fearing *a miniscule moment of witnessing our Nature.*
Many run quick, thinking too highly of themselves.
Others feel outdated, bruised, used, abused,
thinking too little of themselves....
Few find the Goldilocks zone, the Middle Way.
Too much Sun leaves you in a dessert;
not enough, in an Arctic tundra.
The Digital Age seems appropriate for us now,
an external allegory for the complex mechanisms
we walk around with—that we use every day,

yet which most of us have little to no grasp
of how it works and why it is this way....
Running, running, running away from Truth, running
programs like faulty computers on their way out
to the trash heap then the garbage dump.
We can compute trillions and trillions of transactions,
but cannot understand why we keep *reacting*
in the same old way when similar situations arise,
when a certain action is done to us,
or particular words spoken in this or that tone.
Your "free will" *isn't* just given—*pick up the phone!*
We lash out! Then another part of us recoils
at *that* part of ourselves each and every time.
Worse still, we keep fooling ourselves
into believing "the self" which recoils
is the same as "the self" we recoil from that lashes out.
I try to not be cynical or feel defeated from the Sight....
We can send satellites into orbit, yet most of us
cannot even stop ourselves from getting frustrated
by the simple obstacles of existence
(let alone in the true moments of tragedy).
We can build the Freedom Tower to the sky,
yet we cannot find *True Freedom* down here below,
constantly looking for it outside of ourselves,
within the linear perceptions of time. We can climb
mountains, yet sometimes cannot stop
our irrational anger or insatiable hungers
from bubbling up, from sucking us dry,
from making us suck others dry—
all from a situation as simple as misplacing
our keys or our smartphone....
How stupid. How beautiful. How tragic.

We're bothered *too much* or *too easily* by trivial pursuits of little value, and *too little* or *too infrequently* by those of the Highest Value.

For a Childhood Friend

Skateboards, playgrounds, cracking jokes:
small things that seem so much larger now
in passing, in the rearview mirror as
the Wheel of Fortune turns its spokes.
Fists that flew in middle school tore us apart
at a fork in the road we 'ould not control,
setting us down different paths inevitably.
The Hood is harsh. Worn-out streets grab hold,
refusing to let go when it's all we've known.
Some find a way to wrestle out of its grip,
to see beyond it, transformed within grit;
most get eaten up in time, masticated whole,
devoured bit by bit, hit by hit—
as beaten up, suffocating seeds of Soul,
enduring punch after punch, kick after kick.
I'm glad the universe threw us back together
for that brief walk down The Ave last year.
If only I had set some time aside
to visit the barber shop, have you cut my hair....
I truly am sorry that I wasn't there.
With all that seems to float through
our mangled, fractured, fragile minds,
isn't it funny how rarely we ever think,
"Could this be the last time?"—
that someone will find your childhood friend
overdosed on a bathroom floor in a ShopRite.
Wrote to your mom, and said:

"It's strange where the years go,
what they do to us."

Lacuna

Stop shielding yourself from *looking deeper*,
perhaps serving a different purpose
in "doing" so, yet not one that makes us able
to Forge a Path through terrain far from flat.
It's always easier to give up or to give in.
We destroy, forget, misunderstand—
throwing away fuel for our Fire,
just as the burning of Alexandria's
Temple of Knowledge took
a scalpel to the memory of man—
the mechanicalness of things demands
a heavy price for those who wish *to be*.
It's difficult for some to not feel
the absence of all those records and reeds,
the collective memory we expunge
when madness spreads, blights the fields,
grows them again, kills them some more,
spinning the gears of society for centuries.
Recall to recall the Mustard Seeds planted
by those preparing to move on from here, to leave....
Surviving still, Secrets have always been
passed down in whatever garb was required
to hide in plain sight among the multitudes
—when the Sacred Light begins to dim,
Sun sequestered—scattered to the Four Winds,
tucked away in the spaces in-between.
Us wanderers set out by the Light of the Moon.

Tricky Little Devil

Onanism, that Tricky Little Devil,
useless waste of energy
at the wrong time, at the wrong level.
Pleasure for pleasure's sake.
Tricks don't always simply involve
a physical stimulant to dupe:
a pretty thing dangled before me,
la Mujer en la Vestido Rojo—juke!
The road to Sybaris, onerous without
operating, but being operated...
going around in imperfect circles like Satyrs,
a lecherous Silenos drunk on a donkey,
not yet understanding the meaning of Silence.
Pretty ideas can be just as alluring,
especially about oneself.
I've fallen for those p[r]etty traps, too.
Yet it seems some "pleasures" nourish
a pursuit even Higher than what we perceive,
only arising through a particular kind
of consistent, Self-chosen, instructive suffering.
Tricky Devils *do not like this*:
taking from them what's desired
by a constant shedding, shedding, shedding
all the masks of what you think you know
to reassemble the pieces harmoniously
while wading through the Mire,
if the goal is for one to *Grow;* to read
beyond mere speech into Sibylline Speech.

Try feeding *that* pursuit instead,
as difficult as it is to figure out
how to stop oneself in the act.
After all, we have to out-trick a Tricky Little Devil,
depriving it of a tasty meal when it hurts!
In doing so, perhaps we'll graduate, transmuted—
every mask removed.

Warning Road Signs

Beasts with NPD, who evoke unseen entities
in deserts—*workings* with erotic energy—
are more blind than the humble laborers
on these hard streets of wagerers.
It's quite telling that a great "magician",
giving way to almost any perdition,
died a penniless junkie in a flophouse—
his ashes scattered in New Jersey,
of all places....

I'm sure that's *exactly* what Aiwass had in sight
when he told you to live on Cakes of Light—
wiser to *not* simply trust *unknown voices*
inside of one's head, influencing choices.
Just let those dead dogs lay buried down deep.
Do not tread in another's aimless footsteps
that only ever carried seekers further to sleep:
sycophants who call upon voices suspect,
seeking power, then *hear* and *merely accept*!

Such megalomaniacs are certainly a type of fool,
yet not *humble Fools* of the finest quality,
which are always of small quantity.

El Espitu Verde

El Espitu Verde, how you comfort so,
just please leave when I say time to go…

You assist in seeing in new ways, *yes*,
until growing becomes depleted jest
with uncertainty overcoming me
leaving me stuck in one way, at best,
losing the ability to say *no*.

El Espitu Verde, you comfort so,
just leave when I say time to go!

Must realize in myself
to respect this spirit I must not deflect;
that is precisely what it expects.
With my Will, show her the door, then eject.
Build it, brick by brick!

But what about dealing with this reality?
It really hurts....

I know. Trust me, I do.
Such essence is not the only tool.
Knowledge tends to hurt;
understanding brings new peace.
Use Nature's fruits wisely.

Kintsugi: Unoriginal Title of Desperation for Lack of a Better One

No doubt you've been cracked, shattered
many times before if you grasp the gist of this
(if you are desperate enough to *awaken*):
that pristine pottery is far less beautiful,
less durable than those with fractures
filled with purified Silver and Gold,
restored with great care by our own labor
to heal—reconstruct anew—Whole
by unification of each delicate fragment.

A pristine piece of pottery sees itself
as impervious without the realization
that it is not as pristine as it believes
itself to be—that is: precious royal china!
Such pieces will never strive to Strengthen,
to tame the Lion within by holding its maws.
In our reality, there is not such a trifling thing
as a pretty piece of pristine pottery,
only those that *have yet to be tested*
by the Fire, *proven* their worth in Work.
These pieces are looking to be broken.
Only such a piece can be called Precious:
*Nuestra Piedra del Padre y Madre
Despiertos!*

Directional Dyslexia;
Can't Drive You There

Humans are confused creatures;
relationships, complex ships in a sea
without a compass.

How to reach you is a conundrum;
how to help you find the right course,
nearly impossible.

Brothers and Sisters, my Old Friends,
only *you* can navigate your own vessel.
First you have to understand
you are not 'you,' but many 'you's'
that are confused—*used*—
I'd gladly lend *You* a compass
if *i[1]* had One myself.[2]

Still trying to figure out
              which Pieces i require,
                        and how to muster
       the effort needed
to construct
              my own Compass
              out of Compost

---

[1] we
[2] ourselves

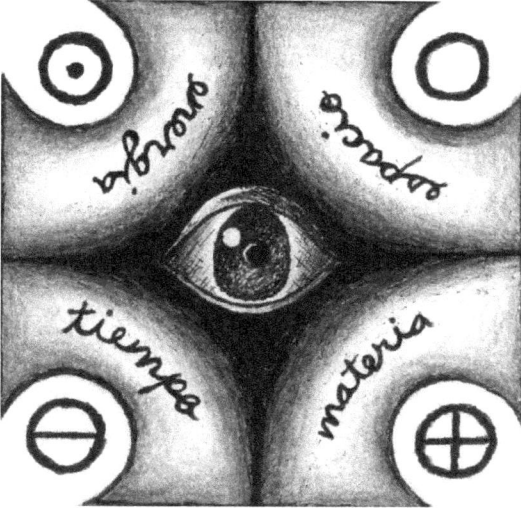

Scatterbrain

Our scatteredness frustrates me. I say *I* will do one thing only to end up "doing" another. No matter how many books are read, or alarm clocks created to *remind me*, the maze feels *eternity-winding*—it never fully quenches the thirst to feel more like an Eagle and less like a rodent rotating in a Yezidi circle, trying to get the damn rats out of my head. From an Enlightened Idiot to an Ordinary One—back to zero and then square one—holding up this Lantern is starting to hurt my damn arm; my fingers actually ache more, even when I drum; my legs aren't what they used to be either; and I'm not what I thought I was. *El cuerpo es pesado, pero el espíritu es Luz Ligero!* Only a year from 30 sun revolutions, still feeling so incomplete (as I suppose I should be)—not taking care of my body well enough—trapped like a piece in a board game of corralled human circus acts and tragi-comedies; a sci-fi-horror-mystery story of silent wars, information wars, psychological wars, and overt bloody wars mixed with slice-of-life everyday drudgery wars, while trying to juggle the responsibilities set before me with staying on the Path. In the moments of silent peace, She says, *"Hold the lantern up anyway!"* That certain 'something' inside me cantillates to *try to see* as much as I can in myself—what is *real*—in other creatures, life-forms, molecules, minerals, the world around us that nourishes the body with its many enticing fruits, yet to distraction—*to be in this world but not of it*—untangle being entangled by these attractions, ingratitude through excess; to avoid abusing that from which we Nurse while seeing everything needed, *all the foods* required in balanced proportions. Pick what is given, yet never to excess, and only what is necessary and produced by your own labors! Don't contribute to drowsily rolling along like locomotive landmines while inside we thrash about in a frenzy, throwing coal into broken furnaces that burst outward into patterns of destructive wars—until the Cosmos shakes, shakes, and shakes us off this planet *again*, declaring:

"Try once more,

idiots!"

Dreams Won't Get You
Up that Mountain, Kid

Did he ever reach
the summit of Mount Analogue?
Did he *see the Center*
between Heaven and Earth
after disease consumed his vessel?
It's difficult to say.
How few of us do in a single lifetime
or even in mortal decay?
Hopefully this Work
will have a proper ending;
that I become complete—
not simply *know* the Center,
but *understand* It with my being
by enduring the pricks and shocks
necessary to get there,
then be strong enough to choose.
Yet hope itself produces nothing,
only dreams of happiness.

And dreams won't get you up that Mountain, kid!

It takes Discipline, Learning, Faith
to build an internal Fire
that burns like all Hell
which will raise you to Heaven.
Down there I build my *Astronave,*
so I can bring it to the summit,

spreading my Wings
into Ethereal Space!

!

Stop yourself right now.
Read this thrice and *feel* it:

I am not what I could be.

That's only the first step.

suggestible

look at the pretty face on screen
trying to convince you

listen to those pretty words
trying to convince you

the pulpit and the pitchfork
the advertisement and the ashram

hypnotic clouds woven with
saccharine ferment painted gold
hang over the heads of us all
a thick fog of suggestibility

telling oneself we aren't
before having honestly looked
only means we are *even more*

Patron Saint of Lost Things, in Boston

The last week of March, in the Gregorian Year of Our Lord, two thousand and nineteen.

We're staying in a little studio apartment on the second floor of 103 Arch Street, across from St. Anthony's Shrine adorned by a massive green-tarnished metallic Christ hanging over the entrance. He seems to loom over us through the window over our bed when we arrived just before midnight. He's tired, nailed up there all year round, forlorn-looking, yet *suffering with so much intent* it's no wonder a symbol like this has been with us as long as this one has. Symbolically, *our* suffering hangs up there. That's our struggle. The choice to make we all want to avoid. That face is the drudgery of everyday life on the surface, but to those who look Below and then Above, it is the conscious suffering absolutely essential on this Path so few discover, let alone set foot on. It is Spirit nailed to sacrificed Matter, then released. If we do not sacrifice Willingly we are eaten up against our will, held prisoner until we learn.

Sat at the windowsill, writing at an awkward angle. I see Him now. I see myself, too. And I see you as well. How easy it is for us to lose ourselves, though—if we ever even 'had' ourselves to begin with....

The following night, stepping outside to smoke a cigarette, I find a dark black man, disheveled, standing suspiciously beside the doorway. Started conversing with him about his life for some reason (instead of just walking up the block to smoke and think to myself, as most people probably would've done). From what I gathered, his years before and after immigrating to the United States from Africa seemed tragic; in and out of prison, says he's trying to get his life back together. After a few minutes, an older white man rides up on a bike, face red and dirty, even more disheveled—ratty, stained baseball cap on his grey head, and a sunken pruned face that seemed to sag toward Hades. In a disgruntled voice this man says he is "looking for a pusher," producing multiple heroin needles from his coat pocket. *Time to go* (hopefully what any rational person would think). *I can do little to nothing for these men right now—or ever, perhaps....*

Doubtlessly catching me off guard, it did not surprise me or shock me necessarily, considering where I come from. I stole a glance at that tired, tarnished Christ and then stamped out my cigarette. The black man offered to sell me some cannabis, which I took a whiff of (out of courtesy when asked) and then respectfully declined. The white man on the bike offered me pills, which I also declined. Told them I already knew my own vices and coping mechanisms. Bid them both goodnight, put the code into the door, and stepped back into the lobby. Deep sigh. Heart racing a bit. Took a moment to gather myself, and then accidentally opened to the door to the wrong bedroom where someone slept in darkness. Thankfully they didn't wake up. Stupid. On my part for lacking awareness after the shock of a strange experience, and on theirs for leaving the apartment door unlocked.

To be frank, I felt more worried about what would

happen if the police approached us than threatened by those two men, ironically enough. Perhaps I have learned to trust them less, despite my pigmentation. In retrospect, I don't recall seeing any police on this street throughout our stay; perhaps it was generally known what goes on amongst those who flock like pigeons around the Shrine at night, wandering aimlessly....

The night after: stood outside with two friends on the corner of Arch and Summer, smoking, and having a discussion about one of the peculiar subjects that interest us. Two men almost broke out into a fight, perhaps ten or twelve feet in front of us, barking at each other in the middle of the road—most likely over some mis-understood exchange of words. They rushed into each others' faces, fists balled up spheres ready to fly (not seeing they were *a piece of Mind tangling with Itself in some fragmentary way for an Unknown Purpose*). After realizing it was all just a misunderstanding, they cooled off, pounded fists in truce, and walked off. I've seen many such interactions before.

We just analyzed, trying to remain unfazed without drawing any unwanted attention, yet still continuing to discreetly discuss what we saw in front of us as it unfolded, vigilant of our surroundings and aware of the *shroud* over these men (and ourselves, to an extent). After finishing our cigarettes, we made our way back to the apartment. As we did, we approached a group of black men huddled in front of the back entrance to the building beside 103 Arch, looking around—*guarding*. In passing, they stared at us angrily, sizing up our intentions; we simply nodded in greeting and I smiled at them. I saw inside of the entryway another man stood facing the wall, hands concealing something near his mouth, with the flame of a lighter aglow…. I knew they must have a planned rotation, taking turns.

Not too long after, the same night: sitting at the windowsill again, my partner and friends behind me laughing in a palaver. A white man and woman come stumbling out of the Shrine of St. Anthony. Difficult to tell their age, especially considering how much of what they were obviously consuming has already deteriorated their brains. Pity welled up instantly. The woman dropped something in the street from a small plastic bag she was handling. Frantically, she threw herself onto the asphalt, picking up the little white bits on her hands and knees. The man threw himself down beside her. Even after every little spec was collected, they continued down the street, crouching low and searching with their cell phone screens for any that could possibly have blown away. There was no breeze that night… just all that false light….

I looked up at Christ a lot during our brief stay (my third visit to "The Cradle of the Revolution") thinking through the labyrinth we exist in—this prison-school of lessons—still feeling both great pity and an unwavering compassion for humanity.

We must not die like dogs, my friends. Anything but that, *if you're reading this and understand the gist of the jest in time!*

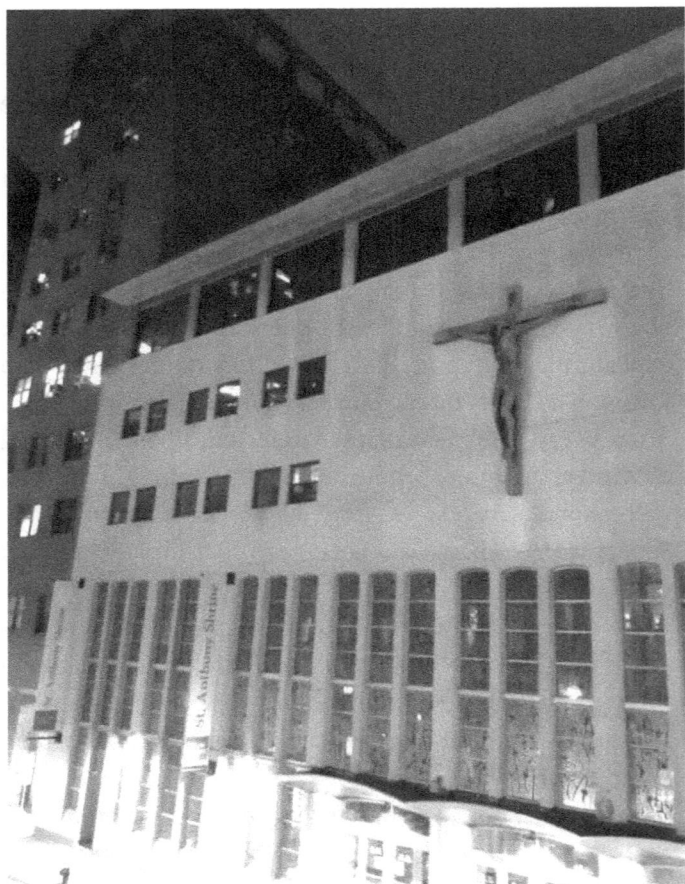

That's the State of the Union
(To Myself *and* My Countrymen)

Dear prosperous entertainment-obsessed anxiety society,

As the poetry and prose of this strange land,
we arose from different regions, from the sands
of time tying us into a devilish dance.
Religions, persecutions, hopes, dreams, demands,
(all similar, all different)—such unusual,
bloody circumstances. Tribalism meets monarchism,
imperialism, colonialism, industrialism, digitalism,
-ism after –ism after –ism, mixed in divisions.
Desperate circumstances. Disparate happenstances.
Greedy aspirations that inevitably lead to nations.
Battling against Nature, ourselves, one another—*you*.
Fine words, fine ideas, slavery, freedom in zoos.
Came up from the soil, came up from the sea,
bled and wed the light and dark hues in me.
That conflict in my blood, *I feel it there*,
hundreds of years in our ground; far and away,
yet somehow still rooted in Jamestown—
the screams of Levi Hicks, shot through the heart,
his skin peeled with a knife from the crown.
But as Kamasi hits my Soul from my speakers now,
only the truly foolish could be blind to such proof
of how wrong we can be, fixating on *external* features.
God's beauty still shines in that saxophone shouting!
We arose from struggles, yet still need rerouting.
Came up with grand ideas along the way, sure,
and many terrible ones, too.... Made strides,

went to the stars... with the help of Nazis and spies.
My ancestors were there, too—I've seen their trace.
Van Pelts in a Civil War, or selling oysters on The Ave.
But my mother was born in Cuba the same exact day
we launched the first American into space,
leaving this floating sphere to explore those stars.
My father's grandfather was Benjamin Franklin Barnes.
Hard to get more American than that shit....
We made so many messes, mistakes. Good men. Fakes.
Fixed other messes, yet made new ones in their place.
Invented the game show, "reality" TV, and the rat race;
shopping malls, Agent Orange, and the atomic bomb.
Reigned terror down in the name of "freedom for all."
Spirit trumped in the Era of Material.
We arose from the struggle. Now we're mostly pouting,
some of us angry we missed the 60's calamities,
living too identified with its drunken hangover,
while others walk around as if none of it ever happened.
Because we always need something to fight for
within the spiritual desert, deposited on these shores.
Hit the books, countrymen. Turn off the TV.
Step away from social media. *Read the great minds*
of all kinds, places, times, hues, races, views.
Then look around you *closely*, and you'll see it, too:
everything decays, making room for growth
from the essence of Soot and Smoke. You'll see
the bones, the blood under our feet, in our genes,
in our heartbeats, in our streets, melodies and beats.
Inside the little boxes on the hillsides, in cold or heat,
along the rivers, or stacked like cubicles full of meat,
which tend to look so pretty on the outside,
yet almost never underneath. You'll see

the suffering never ended within those walls.
The charade simply grew larger in our halls.
Everyone's hiding, distracting themselves, coping.
The masks slip further within; pills in silver tins.
Slaughter never went away, it just became less visible.
It's not about missing the beauty, but seeing the whole,
the nuance, the grey between the extremes.
There's a lot more I could say, obviously,
much of which I've said before—to myself in dreams.
I think whatever the hell this place is now,
we're far away from throwing off King George.
I just wish they would cut the damn budget for war....
Can't help wondering what Adams or Lincoln would say
about the American Experiment, if alive today.
You know things have gone to shit when presidents,
politicians, pundits, celebrities, and cronies toss chips,
hang with perverts on islands, private jets, and ships,
sex-trafficking kingpins dealing children like hits—
drugs for any dark addiction, obsession, or ritual wish.
I can see them in my mind, such dealers among the rich,
dishing helpless beings as products wrapped,
to clientele representative of the most vile, abhorrent
parts of the human specimen that I've mapped.
If slavery ripped the flag in two (and we're still sewing)
the trafficking of the precious and vulnerable remains
an unwavering stain upon the flag's torn remains.
We've made progress healing old wounds, sure,
but creeps creep through Congress, open to any evil lure.
"What flavor do you prefer today?"
that Shadow in them lurking seems to say.
"We have whatever you desire, for whatever twisted way
you are pulled to *live* in the Mire and obey,

43

feeding upon human potential itself
(which you so desperately lack and may never obtain)
through your own effortless existence in Hell.
So here it is, pluck the buds from the vine, then drink.
Buy and sell! Buy and sell! Buy and sell!
Push the entire world to the brink!"
We can do better, I think. Don't let them divide us.
God wants us to look at that side of Him, too....
That's part of how we *get back, by serving through*
Creating, then healing the Old Wounds.
Our potential to develop free will grows
within the mechanicalness that surrounds it whole.
If only we could see beyond the ghettos,
the suburbs, Hollywood and the Hamptons;
the identity fixations, the beautiful things we hide in,
all these damned mass shootings and debates!
If we cannot see *the presence of the Curtain*
between us—the presence of the Veil, and what guards
with strings in horrid hands—then I'm certain
we'll all stumble over the precipice together, man.
It happens sooner or later anyway... so what the hell?
Let me write all of this down, play show and tell.
All great empires eventually evaporate—
the Spirit that first gave it life flies away—
leaving the residue of past ages, some dust scattering,
with the bones in piles in mazes of disarray,
for other generations to pick through.
The Truth remains, a kernel, amongst the chattering.
See the evil lurking in the Halls of Power?
Do your damn duty! See what's in yourself, battling.
Do it by *seeing those hungry Faces in you first.*
After, lift the Lantern to *their* ugly mugs, duly,

because you'll be more prepared to recognize
and know them by their fruits.
And only then should you dare to lift the Lantern
higher than these profane pursuits.
Burn their eyes out with its Glorious Light.
Reveal those parts and predators of the jungle,
then warn the rest of your kin to fight
by telling them to shine their Lights within right.
Remind each and every one who will listen,
"We have already fallen, my fellow Americans.
Maybe we can pick ourselves back up,
but this can't last forever. Did you really believe that?
I'm sorry, friend.... but look at the state of things.
Look at what we have become—where we're at—
armed to the teeth, a powder keg ready to blow
from beneath. Most importantly, look at yourself.
Acknowledge your own faults, all of us fighting over salt,
the part you played when it's all said and done."

Strings are being pulled, left and right.
It feels like many are gearing up for a fight.
Someone's raising the alarms—
the bells are clanging!
While someone else yells, *"Fire, fire!"*
Our hearts start panging. "Who said that?"
No one can tell if it means
someone's shooting at *them*,
if *they* should shoot first,
or if *the whole fucking place*
is actually just burning down.

For Our Lady

Today the Alchemist's Church burns,
the heart of Paris engulfed in flames,
maybe a harbinger of what's to come....
As we stumble backward, enraged,
somnambulant species spiraling out of sync.
I apologize on behalf of us all, Wise Ones,
craftsmen, and laborers of the past.
You saw this coming, though, didn't you?
I wonder if you ever could have predicted
just how much stranger and chaotic
our society would become—
tipping the Scales of Ordered Chaos.
You left behind such massive tomes,
these *Labors of Herakles*, Labors of Love,
with a different mindset in another time,
knowing such signs could only last so long,
knowing how few of us—how *little* within us—
would ever be able to read them,
understand what's hidden in plain sight;
symbols of the past praying, dancing,
suffering, rejoicing, contemplating,
speaking yet maintaining Silence,
frozen in stone pages *trying to hold on*—
in shape, proportion, formulas for *Fé de Fortuna*
further lost in shattered stained glass—
only for these monuments of Higher Thought
to inevitably end up as casualties of our carelessness,
our ruthlessness, our automation—

46

this alone should teach us just as well
about our own place in Merciless Time.
And still, even without understanding,
everyone could *feel* the marvel of such Art—
the time it took to build it, and how long
such a note resonates across the ages—
for all over the world they mourned,
fearing it would be completely lost.
The *true I* mourns in print,
yet still He rejoices!
I never got to experience Her glory, no,
and perhaps I'll see what remains someday,
yet there is a need to honor Her here anyway,
for some reason deeper than words can say.

Honor what does not die,
what cannot simply burn away—
what shapes the stone, fixes the logs in place!
Destroy the roof from which the soul flies;
the Stone foundation still holds firmly in *Place!*

People always rebuild,
perpetually born anew
in Our Lady,

by the Light
of Her Grace.

Headflask

S(He) helps me hold
my lantern aloft with persistence—
illuminating what is down below,
*be*holding the pattern reflected above.
Propped up on a staff on a Path
of twenty-one steps unfolding
in seven layers of infinity;
seeing the nature of batons,
swords, cups, and coins;
of space-time, matter-energy,
flowing from the stuff of Thought—
spoken in an enigmatic effigy
of Light, Number, Form,
Shape, Color, Sound.
Energy, Space, Time, Matter.
Giant little particles in giant little waves
in infinitesimal enormous crucibles.
Mixing the Sol and Luna,
purifying our alloys to *make*
a Child inside of a Headflask,
mirrored in the *mater*ial
at the Beginning and the End—
generously degenerating and regenerating.
Salient chrysalis created internally
through shedding the dross,
beholding the Crux of the Matter.

Three Stories of Mind Fight Inside Me

A chaotic storm churns around a Sacred Mound. Upon this Mound stands *El Gran Palacio*, a royal estate already in disrepair. Inside the Palace, *El Rey Rojo* and *La Reina Blanca* steal away into the highest turret where they discuss which Prince is most fit to rule, who could help them restore order to the estate, its lands, and the lives of their subjects.

With exceeding urgency, the storm has set them in motion; they can no longer ignore what responsibility lies upon the Princes for such a state of affairs, for each inhabits one of three stories of the Palace. *El Rey Rojo* and *La Reina Blanca* discuss how they often feud, forming and breaking alliances with one another, constantly switching sides between each another. Once the parlay was concluded, they decided that in order to test their hypotheses, one by one, the King and Queen would call upon each Prince to ask of them what they themselves thought or felt made them worthy of ruling.

The First and eldest, inhabiting the ground floor of the Palace, barges through the door. When questioned, he becomes angry and begins to argue, *"I follow my gut and my groin, wherever they take me—what else is the point of this? Might as well enjoy ourselves while we're here, right? Just leave me be! There is nothing to discuss here, for I am the rightful heir and all will serve me! I came first, after all!"* He has a powerful Will, yet lacks the Strength to wield it, and in a world of many pleasures and vanities, he would rather *indulge* than have to truly Labor. The First Prince can never find direction or bond with anything for too long, caring little for the subjects or the required upkeep of the kingdom. For him, there's always something new, novel, and delicious to consume, and he becomes enraged when he doesn't get his way.

The First Prince senses the world deeply, yet without emotion, and therefore without a sense of responsibility for his actions.

The Second Prince enters swiftly, seemingly angry, until tears form in his eyes after he is questioned. With reticence, he then replies, *"I follow my heart, which must be the true way to salvation.... I feel at One with everything... with so and so... with God... this will heal me and the world...."* Although his intentions are good, every fleeting positive feeling is mistaken for Love and every negative one dismissed as Evil; his feelings of Oneness absent of calculation become blind, believing a simple way is the only way. He does not see the intricacies of the problems facing their kingdom, and is easily duped and persuaded by his compassion, losing sight of the One and all Its complexities—sometimes enraptured by his rage at injustice. He has great power when he acts, but does not see True Evil lies in his inability to control himself, for when the world does not match what he feels it should be, he can become irrationally angry, indignant, and sorrowful.

The Second Prince feels the world deeply, yet without the critical thought necessary to rebuild.

The Third finally enters upright and proud. When questioned he immediately takes offence and then concludes condescendingly, *"I follow my mind, knowing its*

powerful force to understand and transform the world.
Here *is where we went wrong, and if everyone else just
did* this *or* that *we could change ourselves and the world
for the better! That is the real point of existing, it's for
the sake of....* " He rambles on and on arrogantly. Yet in
incessantly imposing his own fancies upon Creation he
loses the larger picture; in all his categorizations the
Oneness is often missed in the complexity; the inner
depth and interconnectedness of the issues facing their
kingdom go unrecognized. He sees himself as greatest of
all, without question—but all he does is talk and talk,
lacking the Strength and Will to act.

The Third Prince thinks of the world deeply, yet
Aimlessly.

El Rey and *La Reina* find it is exactly as they feared.
Their observations and initial concerns were confirmed
after hearing each of their responses. They decide rather
than one of the Princes ruling *El Gran Palacio*, that
perhaps all Three should rule as partners. If only the
Princes could learn to cooperate instead of fighting, then
perhaps they would remember that they are all kin who
must share this Home, setting it in order. What else is
there to do once they come to realize that each has
something the other needs to be complete and rule
justly? Otherwise, none of them will ever *truly* rule at
all, recreating their world anew.

When *El Rey Rojo* and *La Reina Blanca*, the *Royal
Rebus*, step in to mediate by granting the Princes an
Aim, let each of these Princes be candid; let them com-
municate with one another their individual wants and
needs, improve one another, become a Balance of
Powers. They will see how *invulnerable they can be-*

come together by first seeing how *truly suggestible they are apart*, catching each other *in the act of acting* against the Household; holding each other accountable. This is a difficult conflict to resolve, a careful process conducted in a laboratory deep inside the basement of *El Gran Palacio*; in the darkness of night; in the eye of an inevitable storm. If they could begin to work together in *harmony* rather than against one another, balancing their respective needs with their individual responsibilities, then perhaps *El Gran Palacio* can be set in order from the foundation up, with all of the lands replenished and subjects cared for.

The Three Princes *may* become One Master of One Household, giving birth to a precious Treasure, but as the King and Queen assured them: "It will require a great deal of labor and a great deal of patience to become balanced like us, and thus give birth to the *filius philosophorum!*"

Maybe this is what he meant when a wise alchemist once sang to us in printed secrets, "And so it is likewise necessary in the Philosophic work that these Three Fathers should seem to Conspire together for the Birth of one offspring, that is to be the Darling of the Philosophers."

The Whole Man

Mount your donkey, ride it consciously.
You'll trip and fall on your ass a few times,
so leave a thread behind you on the Road
toward the Crossed Keys that decipher the marks
left behind outside and inside
of whoever Works to decipher. To remind them
and yourself. Most won't hear you;
the rest will hear you speaking in idiotic tongues.
The vulgar who spot you on the Way will see you
riding ass-backward, only to point, laugh, and say,
"Look how stupid he looks riding so absurdly!"—
never understanding the compromise,
why you have erected this circle around yourself.
They may even cast you out with stones and shards.
Leave such signposts, nonetheless; *an X*
to mark the spot, as 'they' say,
where Treasure is surely found! It's useful
for others who will come after you to stumble
over these pebbles in a pile where you once stumbled—
so demonstrate for them by riding ass-backward!
Show them the truth in excrement,
if that's all they see, after all. I jest, of course.
But those who understand, who catch my drift?
Who see what can be extracted from this devilishness?
I'll meet you There, my friends!
We'll subdue The Beast together,
dance upon his grave.

Maybe if I Work *diligently*,
perhaps you will be more inclined—
if I can destroy—expel—the shit in myself first,
everything I imagine I am, want to be or can—
tell myself and others I am, or know, understand….
When I arrive in the Middle, I'll tie Her thread
to an Oak Branch in joyful celebration;
sacrifice *myself to Myself* on Odin's Gallows—
say *I* and truly mean it *in that choice.*
And if you should happen upon these footsteps,
spotting me on the Way in front of you—
I'll be *here* facing you directly, saying "Come along!
Triumphantly together in our solitary brotherhood
we can *remember* the Lost Word; *grow* the Eyes to See;
speak in One Tongue; *obtain* Our Wings to Fly;
create things of worth in good Faith,
instead of making more *miedra to learn from
then flush*—sputtering more Babel into the wind,
into the void that is a part of Reality, too:
the Grotesque Face of God that *must be recognized,
contended with, looked upon directly*
—as the water slowly erodes it all away—
without turning to stone to become a Stone
(if we aren't blinded by the Light and driven mad first)."

Truly I say, approach the Shrine to call upon Her name.
Place yourself in a coffin carried by pastophori
and be liberated from the past in these passuses,
until shedding the heavy asinine form
onward to Greener Pastures!
The fission at the Center of the Maze is arduous,
so only the Will of Odin, the Courage of Theseus,

the Quickness of Hermes,
can brush away the dark pigments to reveal
the entire painting—the Whole Man, Illuminated!
Solitarily we arrive *together* to gather Our Fruit
from the Great Trees of Hesperides,
meeting again as Old Friends among the Branches
chirping away the Heropass in eternal discourse.

La Puerta de la Muerte

...ripening transitions into rotting,
after having danced from a Spark into green,
a beginning and ending of Single Mind's Dreams

some *venture*

yet not to say for sure what lies beyond the Door
as green moves to black, and then more—
we all find out Soon enough...

Death Says to the Outcast, "Pick a Stool!"

They say a fear of Death is natural.
We never find out who "they" are, but
it's no wonder it is dreadful to overcome,
for we are beings rooted half in Nature
from which and to which this form goes.
She's how we all survive—how we arrive,
how we interpret through "I"—how we die.
Part of our predicament is *not* thinking about it
often enough, unless faced with mortal danger.
Then there's thinking about it *too much*,
too imaginatively, unnecessarily.
I've shed tears just thinking of you dying.
Shivered to a core that cannot be named
thinking of my own death—maimed,
others have shed blood to meet Death,
or to stop it, avenge it, even serve it.
The Scythe is an indiscriminate motivator;
how we respond to the prodding
of the blade is the Mystery!
For we have the ability to reach beyond—
hacia el Cielo en la vida!
Discover the meaning of True Freedom.
To be something other than
that which grovels in the dirt,
follows incited instinct, pure pleasure;
we can delay gratification if necessary:
for loved ones, for posterity.
sacrifice the present for a possible future,

suffer consciously for a deliberate purpose.
Perhaps the fear of dying can also be slain
for a deliberate purpose to rise to the surface,
a step toward a new Birth in Death
which physically itself cannot be stopped here,
only consciously prepared for
by seeing its paradoxical illusion
yet essential reality *without flinching*.
I'm not certain I've stopped myself
from flinching each time.
Yet I know there is a Dying Before Dying.
Despite this obvious fact,
something in me *has begun to die*—
a "me" that *wants to go back to sleep*—
making room out of ashes, out of uncertainty:
a certain 'something' remains
which cannot simply stay in bed,
because It sees there is no going back...
It often says, *"Get out from under those covers,*
fly like an arrow, then die standing akimbo—
not tranquilly in your sleep!"
Now I hear the swish of the Scythe
say along the Way:

"Pick a stool!
Have a seat and stay awhile, kid.
Two places to sit,
two ways of arriving in my arms:

"The first stool is beautifully upholstered,
comfortable beyond compare, in fact,
although inside it is rotting, collapsing.

Sit here and you will die having put off
the pain of looking at yourself,
feasting upon the sweets of the earth,
but suffering terribly later, regardless,
and gaining little to nothing in return....

"The second Stool is filled
with Gold and Silver inside,
but the outside is covered in sharp ostraka
poking your ass, reminding you of its presence,
which will puncture you and even be thrown at you
by others who may see you sitting so absurdly—
until you testify to all of the stool churning inside
yourself trying to hide, making everyone sick—
coming out in buckets until you are cast out!
If you sit there and stew in that for awhile,
although you will suffer much now
you will gain something in return
of far more value in the end!
A Star that may signal
Your success!

"Most have 'chosen' the first stool,
in a sense, because they were born sitting there
and it's the only way they know how to sit,
overlooking the second and Its Veritable Value.
Very few have even really seen the other Stool,
let alone chosen to sit in such a grotesque manner,
and when they do, they are rarely understood
by anyone around them—often ridiculed,
or even perceived as heretical, doom and gloom,
far removed, and always up to no good.

Both sitters will suffer greatly at My Hand—
one in the long-run and the other immediately
by choice to Rejoice later in Holy Knowledge.
But worst of all is he who has truly seen
the second Stool (which is actually the First!)
yet tries to remain comfortable
on the one he was born sitting on
while realizing it's collapsing on the inside;
fighting to ignore that hideous, decrepit,
sharp thing guarding the Center—
such a man is the most miserable of all."

Inside the Maze, Apterous and Afraid

Each of us who travel along this Road, incalculable
winding, lifting an ever-present load, the material—
trying to crack the Code, in all times,
all places, all modes—
with a stick and a donkey's back,
and a shell on our hats. I see many of you
above me on the slopes, climbing
with ease upon blazing ropes,
when just the rocks alone are hurting
my hands, my feet, my bones....
and I feel overwhelmed,
swerving, undeserving. often alone....
I honestly suck at this....

(There's room for improvement.)

Sometimes there's a clear place to walk.
Sometimes none in sight. I'm lost.
Forget forced structure
or the clever turn of phrase....
My patience is underdeveloped,
I keep tripping over myself,
or falling off my donkey onto my back.
And then I kick the damn thing, injuring myself
like the idiot I know I am,
letting itself be pulled here and there
—vulnerable little child, kicking and screaming,
yelling out at the seemingly uncaring universe in anger

as if there's any apparent concern at all for my own
mistakes—as if it was so easily clear
that there's *any real reason at all* for my circumstances,
for anything (and who's to say what's "real"?)
other than to learn a harsh Truth, to not be a meal
—we know such a concern, an unwinding,
is our own damn job to figure out—
why the hell else would we have been given
'consciousness' to any degree, you fool?

(See, you do *know this!)*

Yet I'm still limping along in my own shame.
Losing my temper, dropping it in a well,
forgetting, forgetting, forgetting... wanting to lose
my name—the kid-me losing at video games,
chucking the controller across the room.
Not what I'm supposed to be. I'm not. I'm not. I'm no—

(What you could *be! Have patience.)*

Still don't have control...
dwelling on it, dwelling on it, dwelling.
Looping mental states.
Until I hate myself more for lacking it
and then get sucked into *that* loop, too!
Christ, what a tricky process this shit is!
These transformations....

(Alright—enough!
Grow the Hell up
and stop whining like a coward,

64

spilling seemingly private information with a glower.)

—or I can go back to forced rhyming, at least—
—that would sound prettier and less shitter, at least—
—or go back to simpler, at least....

it'll sell
more books, at least
I'll enjoy more fine dining,
at least—restore
the peace for a moment,
at least—just a little....

(More whining.
Let me know when you cool off,
and silence the Beast
when attention is required
to be increased.)

Will I take advantage of *any* of this and learn?
If not, hopefully you do,
at least.

Damn it all....

We need to *Burn!*

(Back to the books.
Keep studying. The world still turns.)

GARGOYLE
GETTINGS
MUTUS
BERGERAC
THE
HISTORY OF CARICATURE AND OF GROTESQUE IN ART. WRIGHT

Calcination:
An Attack on My Self-Importance

Stop with the proselytizing
and the self-flagellations!
That is not the point of this.

The point is to beat myself
over the *head* with it.
And there's nothing in here anyone
could ever be *'converted'* to, anyway....
The Lead that must be converted
lies buried within every person.
It's easy to find it, but not easy to refine it.
I wouldn't ask that of you anyway.
But I still need more reminders to me:
When you are not yet ready to teach,
perhaps you can only teach others by showing
your own process of learning.
Your own level of being.

Thus I make an ass out of myself,
hoping others might see *that 'something' Divine*
in themselves, too. Here it is—
I babble at the birds, trying to understand them.
Take it or leave it.

If you take it:
Extract!

The Reds

Finally spotted a blue jay

(alive this time)

fly over the red rose bush in the backyard.
Descended the steps quickly to be sure—

for a better look:

He perched on the fence, tall, proud, erect,
in the shade while the Sun was sulfur hot.
Within a second, he flew from my world,

wings swift, mercurial.

If only he would come around
more often to make me
recall the return of such ruby reds,
tying us all together

in a lemniscate between two poles
of hot and cold, presence and absence

perceived.

The blue jays amongst the cardinals,
Blue Hues within the Reds of roses
ALL housed in Green.

For the Drooping Willow Weighed Down by Sleep: *"Awaken!"*

Dear friend, here's the true value of all this bullshit:

What *in the Hell* did you discover down here,
while wading through the Mire of all your woes,
drooping your leaves so low to the ground below?
Lingered too long in the thick mud of self-hate?
What did you learn from the tests? From the weight?
And by what do you actually weigh yourself and why?
By pounds? By appearance? By mental gymnastics?
By your turn of phrase, a need to demonstrate?
To make you feel worthier of praise, love, validation?
What about by what you can create, then give back?
Get out of your own way. Pick up the damn shovel,
put some legwork into it—don't strain your back!

Hate your body, *it will never cooperate with you.*
Hate your emotions, *they will rule over you forever.*
Hate your mind, *it will surely continue to malfunction.*
Hate the world, *they will always feel like your enemies,*
rather than other versions of yourself wading with us.

Please hear me, Drooping Willow:
Cut the albatross of envy from your branches,
and raise them just a little higher toward the Sun.

Sometimes I also need reminding.
That's why I wrote this.

Re*fine*

What so-called big shots and critics think
matters little to me here, hence why I do *this* shit alone.
  Blunt, I know. The New Jerseyan in me cares not.
I let him out sometimes when he's useful to wear.
  But please take me apart forever. Rip me to shreds.
We'll both get more out such banter if you do.
  Better that than an indifferent robotic silence.
Crucify me three times; three times to rise.
  Elevarse como el Fénix! Mas cera del Cielo!
Lo siento, I'm still working on my Spanish....
  But once I see myself *accurately* enough (control
my inner sense of doom; clean my damned room)
  I may have as much mastery of my existence
as I *know* must be obtainable, to ever-adjust—
  to throw on and off any role needed outside,
find the purest Gold and the finest Silver
  from down within the Salt of the Mind,
yet never be too identified with any of the masks
  in this maze of many corridors to wind
—especially my own name, my own time—
  make art for Art's sake, then *change!*   *Unwind!*
Maybe then I'll write better material, too,
  until one day I embrace a *content spoken Silence.*
Remake. Send it out. Learn from it. Let go.   Refine.
  In the end, it has only ever been You, hasn't it?
Conscious Faith with a capital F, Divine—

a *conscience* born in a fortress of eternal Designs
which, in the end for us, tear off every Disguise,
   as in the arms of Death we face the True Trial
of *holding Oneself together* in brilliant Light
   while beholding the great Shadow it casts!
Woe to all who seek only to take, take, take on
   this Path *for power*, but who will not pre*serve*—
the Mighty Maw will suck you dry, unmake!
   We *will* get what we deserve....

II

In the Forge of Hephaestus, I forge these pages.
   All I know for sure is: DNA is a language—
      that we are fundamentally information,
all of us—in a Web. Therefore I love you. regardless.
And that esoteric knowledge flows from One Source,

yet through many Streams

into an external world of illusions, nightmares, dreams,
   mirroring the internal world of finding purpose,
where nothing is what it appears to be on the surface.
When I'm "gone," at my funeral play Coltrane's *Olé.*
   Think of me in its sway, passing along in rhythm
beyond what these ephemeral words can even convey.
I wrestled bulls while I was here, Minotaurs in a Maze,
   trying to re<u>fine</u> myself before the end of my days.
      Remember me in death's arms that way.

One final reminder to myself: *Earn this!*
Kill the flowery language dreams of glamour

(to make your Garden of Words an entire Ecosystem)

by placing your head inside of this Furnace:
always think, think, think with a hammer!

Get your ass to the Middle
—even if it takes more than one lifetime—
just don't forget to set yourself on Fire!

+

Blend
each center.
Deconstruct and
reconstruct myself. Stop
all their incessant bickering!
There *is One in there* Who *knows*
how to bring them all together
under a Single Roof; Who can
grow enough *being* which
holds the *understanding*
from Above. Yet they
keep shouting at Him to
shut the Hell up—leave us!
grant Heaven without Work!
I must find the Primary Colors
and mix the pigments necessary
to see with Vision. Then read the Signs
of Winged Ones where we find guidance;
struggle to throw off all vanities, all illusions inside;

struggle
with my inner Devil!
Such is the true *Foundation Stone*
from which the initial energy needed
arises to heat the Hermetic Furnace,
where the grotesque *first matter*
is found; the Great Teachers
have always insisted
it was so.

Daniel de la Fé (b. 1990) is an American writer, poet, artist, and musician from Elizabeth, New Jersey, spending much his time in the Hell's Kitchen neighborhood of New York City. This is his fourth book of poetry.

"All religions speak about death during this life on earth. Death must come before rebirth. But what must die? False confidence in one's own knowledge, self-love and egoism. Our egoism must be broken. We must realize that we are very complicated machines, and so this process of breaking is bound to be a long and difficult task. Before real growth becomes possible, our personality must die."

—Gurdjieff, from *Views from the Real World*, pg. 86

"No man is a prophet in his own country. Perhaps this old saying gives the occult reason for the convulsion produced in the solitary and studious life of a philosopher by the flash of Revelation. Under the influence of that divine flame, the former man is entirely consumed. Name, family, native land, all the illusions, all the errors, all the vanities fall to dust. And, like the phoenix of the poets, a new personality is reborn from the ash. That, at least, is how the philosophic Tradition would have it."

—Eugène Canseliet, Preface to the First Edition
of *Le Mystere des Cathedrales,* Fulcanelli,
trans. Mary Sworder, pg. 6

"As the sun and each atom of ether is a sphere complete in itself, yet at the same time only a part of a whole too vast for man to comprehend, so each individual bears within himself his own purpose, yet bears it to serve a general purpose unfathomable to man."

—Leo Tolstoy, "Second Epilogue", *War and Peace,*
trans. Ann Dunnigan